Get Your Life Today

7 Success Hacks for Life, Leadership, and Business

A Companion

Journal

Desiree Cocroft

Get Your Life Today

How To Get Your Life With This Journal

I am excited about the change that you are going to experience because you decided to do something different! You are making a choice to invest in your life through using this journal and having the "Get Your Life Today" book be your guide!

The purpose of this journal is to be a "homebase" for the reflection that you will have and the actions you will take as you read "Get Your Life Today." Answer the writing prompts and take the necessary actions to get the results you want in your life.

This is not just about writing things down. It is about getting what is in you OUT! First, you will get it out of your head and on paper. Then, it will be your duty to make the moves necessary to see what is on paper come to life... in real life.

Are you ready?!

It's time to go and be great!

> # "

What's the world for if you can't make it up the way you want it?

TONI MORRISON

Introduction

The World Is Waiting on the Bigger Version of You

Remember <u>this</u>:

- There is a bigger version of you that you can become starting today.

- You get to lean into the disruption that comes to either hinder you or catapult you. Choose to be catapulted.

- The fear factor will always be present. It will never completely go away, so you might as well go BIG anyway. Choose BIG.

REFLECTION QUESTIONS:

1. What is the biggest version of yourself?

2. What have you wanted to explore, but were too afraid to pursue?

3. What people do you believe are "waiting" for you to serve them? What do they look like?

____

____

____

____

____

____

____

____

____

#SUCCESS HACKS: PRE-WORK

Life: Showing up differently for your family and relationships is huge. Think about what the biggest version of yourself as a spouse, a parent, a friend, and a family member would look like. Take steps to embody that each day.

Leadership: Attitude follows leadership, and leadership happens one decision at a time. Think about the role model you are in your organization. Are you being the best version of yourself as it relates to leading, developing others, and achieving your team's highest goals?

Business: Look at your business. Is it operating with the biggest version of it in mind, or are you playing small? It may not be the biggest version right now, but are you strategically setting it up to be most impactful to your customers and the world?

BONUS ACTIVITY: Create a Personal Mission

Create a personal mission statement that reflects who you are and the impact you want to have. Use the template on my website (www.desireecocroft.com/mission) to create your mission statement! Keep it, refine it, post it, and use it . . . That means say it out loud!

____

____

____

____

____

____

____

____

____

____

____

I used to want the words
‘She tried’ on my tombstone. Now I
want ‘She did it.’

KATHERINE DUNHAM

Chapter 1

Confidence Comes When You Decide

Success Hack # 1

Remember <u>this</u>:

- Confidence doesn't come in idleness. It comes when you make a decision AND take action on it.

- Even if you fail, you can learn more from doing. Decide to DO, and then make adjustments as necessary.

- We tend to be so critical of ourselves that we speak out of our deficiencies. Choose to speak out of your strengths.

REFLECTION QUESTIONS:

1. What are some of your personal strengths?

2. How often do you communicate your strengths to others?

3. Think of something that you want to accomplish; how can you speak from your strengths?

____

____

____

____

____

____

____

____

____

____

#SUCCESS HACKS

Life: Decide that your personal life will be better by moving on a decision that you have hesitated to make happen. Perhaps it is changing your eating habits or spending more time with your family. Either way, make a decision, and the steps to getting there will come.

Leadership: Think about conversations that are necessary to have with one of your employees. If you are feeling intimidated around having a crucial conversation, first decide that having the conversation is necessary for forward movement. Then, make the first step by scheduling an appointment to chat with your employee.

Business: Procrastination in making important business decisions can hinder your growth. If you are anxious about pursuing a new revenue stream or making a change to your business model, consider what will be the biggest bang for your buck. Choose to move forward in that area, and the resources that you need will be clear.

"

If I didn't define myself for myself, I would be crunched into other people's fantasies for me and be eaten alive.

"

AUDRE LORDE

Chapter 2

Define Your Success

Success Hack # 2

Remember <u>this</u>:

- Refine and define. As you refine your mission over time, define your success.

- Other people's success does not have to be your measure of success. You decide what you want your path to look like.

- If you don't define your success, you will default to someone else's definition for you. Get grounded on what you believe you are called to do and be open to how it can look.

REFLECTION QUESTIONS:

1. What does success look like in line with your mission statement?

2. If you could describe the "how" of fulfilling your mission, what would it be?

____

____

____

____

____

____

____

____

____

#SUCCESS HACKS

Life: When you look around, you will see so many examples of success. Define what success in these areas looks like for you: in relationships, physical health, spiritual, financial, career, and mental health. How will you know you are experiencing success in these areas?

Leadership: Remember, mission without definition doesn't mean much! After discovering your mission, take time to think about how you want to be defined as a leader. How will you know you are a successful leader based on your core values?

Business: Your business is yours. In defining your business, it is important to "mind yo business" (pun intended). What is success in your business through your eyes? Define how you will know your business is successful.

I have discovered in life
that there are ways of
getting almost anywhere
you want to go, if you really
want to go.

LANGSTON HUGHES

Chapter 3

You Have Everything You Need

Success Hack # 3

Remember <u>this</u>:

- You have everything you need internally, and your results are the proof!

- You have everything you need externally, between the people you know, the ones you haven't met, and your mama, Google.

REFLECTION QUESTIONS:

1. What are the accomplishments that you have in your life that you have overlooked?

2. Who do you know that has access to or can refer you to the resources you need?

____

____

____

____

____

____

____

____

____

____

#SUCCESS HACKS

Life: When we take time to get over ourselves, we see that we have everything that we need to be great. What do you already have to see yourself achieve success in your relationships, physical health, spiritual, financial, career, and mental health?

Leadership: If you get down to some basic principles, then you may notice that you have some key characteristics that you can use as a foundation for your leadership growth. Focusing on your strengths can allow you to blossom more than when you speak out of your deficiencies. Take a survey of your personal strengths and think about how your ability to develop leaders can be more impactful!

Business: Do you have a team of people? If you said yes, how can the team be refined to meet your company goals? If you answered no, how can you build a team based on the greatest gaps in your business? Start with your biggest need gap, define what success in that area would look like, and employ someone, even if it is a short-term contract.

I prayed for twenty years but received no answer until I prayed with my legs.

FREDERICK DOUGLASS

Chapter 4

Take Big Baby Steps

Success Hack # 4

Remember <u>this</u>:

- Be like Speedy: take a chance, stretch yourself, and be OK with falling. Just take a quick cry and get back up!

- Choose the biggest bang for your buck to focus on and then choose big baby steps to achieve it.

- Your big baby step is not everyone else's step. Do what will stretch, excite, and resonate with you.

- Stay consistent with your steps and have a measure of success.

REFLECTION QUESTIONS:

1. What is the focus area that would be the biggest bang for your buck?

2. What big baby step is the one that stretches and excites you most?

3. What is your measure of success (choose a number: date, money, weight, hours, days off, etc.)?

#SUCCESS HACKS

Life: If you have only been taking safe tiny steps, then I want you to think of how you could take uncomfortable, big steps in your relationships, physical health, spiritual, financial, career, and mental health. Go do ONE thing in the area that you are most concerned about. Make it a BIG baby step.

Leadership: Have you truly stretched yourself? If not, consider your definition of success as a leader. What is one BIG baby step you can take to catapult your leadership development so you can create leaders in your organization?

Business: Are you half-stepping in your business? Are you choosing medium action steps? Remember, it's OK to have small goals, but my question is does it challenge you? If not, scare yourself a bit. Choose an action that will make you show up differently in your business. Go BIG baby!

> ## What you're thinking is what you're becoming.

MUHAMMAD ALI

Chapter 5

Get Your Mind Right and Your Game Tight

Success Hack # 5

Remember <u>this</u>:

- Your mind has to shift if you want to have different outcomes.

- Use the lies, the truth, and the proof to shift your thinking.

- Keep the party going by feeding your mind daily bread to maintain your new identity.

- Keep your positive emotions high so you can stay balanced. Negative emotions aren't always bad. They are sticky, and we need more positive emotions to stay balanced.

REFLECTION QUESTIONS:

1. What new identity do you need to adopt to move into better results in your life?

2. Who will you empower to help stay accountable for your shift?

____

____

____

____

____

____

____

42

#SUCCESS HACKS

Life: Are you limiting your greatness because of your perspective? Think about what you find yourself saying about your relationships, physical health, spiritual, financial, career, and mental health. How are your thoughts holding you back? What could you give yourself permission to believe?

Leadership: How do you perceive yourself as a leader? How are your thoughts holding you back from being greater? What beliefs about yourself do you need to adopt to see your biggest version of yourself? How would it look to walk in those beliefs each day?

Business: How have you limited the growth of your business with simply your thoughts of what is possible? What if you had limitless possibilities? How would you show up in your business then?

"

No person is your friend
who demands your silence,
or denies your right to
grow.

ALICE WALKER

Chapter 6

Build Your A-Team

Success Hack # 6

Remember <u>this</u>:

- Your A-Team is to help you have a circle of people around that support the growth in your life both personally and professionally.

- Re-evaluate your team. Change expectations. Remove people and add people to the proper areas of your life.

- Get a mentor or an additional mentor!

- Be the person you want to attract.

REFLECTION QUESTIONS:

1. How will new relationships benefit you right now?

2. How can you have more authentic experiences with people in your circle?

3. How can you set clear expectations and boundaries with people in your life?

____

____

____

____

____

____

____

____

____

____

#SUCCESS HACKS

Life: Think about the version of yourself that you are stepping into in this season of life. Who in your life will be on your A-Team to support that life? Who are those folks that may remain in your life, but will no longer be your "go-to" for encouragement or progress in your relationships, physical health, spiritual, financial, career, and mental health? Reach out to those that you want to add. Refrain from having conversations that are not beneficial with those who are not meant to be in your inner circle support.

Leadership: Toxic relationships will do you no good as you are developing leaders in your organization. Take a survey of those in your inner circles. Create an A-Team that will be in sync with who you are becoming.

Business: How can you create an A-Team type of business environment? What systems can you begin to introduce in your workspace to encourage an A-Team culture?

> You never know which experiences of life are going to be of value... You've got to leave yourself open to the hidden opportunities.

ROBIN ROBERTS

Chapter 7

Loving the Journey is the Destination

Success Hack # 7

Remember <u>this</u>:

- Your life is a good movie. Enjoy every part of it without rushing through it.

- Use gratitude each day to love your journey no matter what you may be experiencing in life.

- Savor the moments you love like a good meal.

- Be decisive so that you enjoy more of the outcomes of your decisions without delay.

REFLECTION QUESTIONS:

1. What part of your journey do you need to appreciate more?

2. What type of decision-making changes do you need to adopt to be a satisficer?

____

____

____

____

____

____

____

#SUCCESS HACKS

Life: How will you choose to celebrate your success on your journey to the biggest version of yourself? Remember, each BIG baby step matters! Sprinkle a little happiness each step of the way! When you hit a fail, because you will, how will you respond in a way that allows you to love your journey?

Leadership: How will you embrace your growth opportunities as you become the biggest version of yourself as a leader? What would it look like to give yourself grace along the way?

Business: How can you celebrate taking action in your business consistently? No matter the numbers, how can you use each time you grow as a reminder that you are one step further than the day before? What simple strategies can you put in place to give yourself space to enjoy your journey as an entrepreneur?

Conclusion

I leave you with this quote below as you move forward to getting your life today:

"

A life is not important except in the impact it has on other lives..

"

JACKIE ROBINSON

Someone is on the other end of you saying "yes" to who you know you are to become. They are waiting to see and be served by you. Their greatness is connected to yours. Your story, even with all of its problems, was formed to be a solution for their life. Get your life today so they can be empowered to get their life tomorrow.